LEGACY OF PRAYER

LEGACY OF PRAYER

A SPIRITUAL TRUST FUND FOR THE GENERATIONS

Jennifer Kennedy Dean

New Hope Publishers

Birmingham, Alabama

New Hope Publishers
P. O. Box 12065
Birmingham, AL 35202-2065
www.newhopepubl.com

Library of Congress Cataloging-in-Publication Data

Dean, Jennifer Kennedy.
  Legacy of prayer : a spiritual trust fund for the generations / by Jennifer Kennedy Dean.
     p. cm.
  ISBN 1-56309-711-7 (pbk.)
  1. Parents—Religious life. 2. Intercessory prayer—Christianity. I. Title.
  BV4529 .D43 2002
  248.3'2—dc21
                                        2001007691

Unless otherwise noted, all Scripture references are from the *New International Version*. Copyright © 1973, 1978, 1984 International Bible Society. Used by permission of Zondervan Bible Publishers.

Cover design by Righteous Planet, Nashville, Tennessee

ISBN: 1-56309-711-7

N024119 • 0502 • 6.5M1

One generation shall praise Your works to another, and shall declare your mighty acts.

—Psalm 145:4 NKJV

TABLE OF CONTENTS

INTRODUCTION

As parents, we give careful thought and attention to providing for our children. Would a mother send her young child out into the cold without a coat and hat? Would a father forget to feed his children? Knowing their dependence on us for protection and provision, our hearts are attuned to our children's physical and emotional needs. In many cases we know their needs even before they do, and fulfill their needs before they ask.

If we would give such careful attention to our children's physical safety and emotional well-being, why would we ever send them out without a spiritual covering? The most important provision we can make for our children is to provide for their spiritual prosperity.

Just as we daily provide food, shelter, clothing, love, and discipline for our children—all their needs—we can also cover them daily with prayer, providing an ongoing provision for their welfare. Prayer not only operates in the spiritual realm; it also brings the power and provision of God into the material realm. By saturating our children's lives in prayer, we activate God's will in every realm of their lives.

Prayer has no limits—no time limits, no geographical limits. Just as surely as we can provide for our children's present and daily needs through prayer, we can also reach into their futures, laying a foundation of blessings for our children, our grandchildren, and all of our descendants.

Prayer is so effective that when our children are away from us, we can continue to parent them through our prayers. Our prayers are more powerful even than our presence.

What parent does not hope to leave his or her child an inheritance—a nest egg—to make that child's life richer and easier? How many parents, in fact, struggle and work with just this goal in mind?

And yet the results of such efforts will vary. It's possible to leave behind wealth or a business, and then have a natural or economic disaster sweep away that storehouse in just a day. Some have left large domains to descendants, who then squander in a few years what took several lifetimes to accumulate. Some heirs find the very wealth they inherit to be their destruction.

It may be wonderful to leave behind wealth for the generations to follow. But at best, money and possessions are fragile and unstable. However, *we can* leave behind for our descendants a spiritual trust that can never be stolen, squandered, or lost. We can leave riches that will only increase in value. We can lay up a store of imperishable wealth.

"Do not store up for yourselves treasures on earth, where moth and rust destroy, and where thieves break in and steal. But store up for yourselves treasures in heaven, where moth and rust do not destroy, and where thieves do not break in and steal."

—Matthew 6:19–20

In this statement, Jesus used one of His favorite teaching devices: He pointed to an earth-picture to illustrate a spiritual reality. He calls our attention to the fact that we store up wealth on earth. We save it. We invest it. We work and expend energy to accumulate it, and we exercise discipline to lay it aside for generations to come.

The same principle applies to spiritual riches. You can store them up and put them on deposit for generations to follow. As you study this book, you will learn how to make deposits in the spiritual realm for those who come behind.

Never Too Late

If you are saying, "It's too late. My children are grown," wait! Don't give up. Some of you did not even know Christ when you were raising your children. You didn't know to pray for them. If your children and grandchildren are unbelievers, you may think it's your fault. Don't put this book aside. Begin now to pray for your children, grandchildren, and descendants.

What if you just came into great material wealth? Would you say, "Well, it's too late for this wealth to benefit my children, either now or for the future. If only I'd had this abundance when they were younger!"? No! You would begin now to lavish it on them and invest it for their futures.

God was operating in your children's lives even before you knew to pray for them. He heard then the prayers you would someday pray. You will see, when the end of His story is told, that God has always been laying the groundwork for your children to come to know Him.

Spiritual Parents

Maybe you are not a parent in the traditional way. No one calls you "Mom" or "Dad." Maybe, instead, God has intersected your life with children in other ways: teacher, friend, aunt, uncle, coach. In fact, maybe this very issue causes you grief. Has God impregnated your heart with a great love for children, teenagers, or young adults? If so, then He has given you a love that can cause your prayers to flow for these individuals. Like Paul, you can say, "My dear children, for whom I am again in the pains of childbirth until Christ is formed in you" (Galatians 4:19). Will you open your heart and your life fully to those whom God has given you? (Galatians 4:27)

Some of you are still in your childbearing years and are walking through the tremendous pain of infertility. Don't give up. Yield yourself to the One who has created in you a deep desire for children. Your longing to have children is the echo of God's own heart. Let your experience teach you how He yearns over each of us until we are born again into His family.

The Lord has placed a prayer in me that I pray for couples who are having trouble conceiving, and I pray it for you now: *Lord, let the baby that she holds in her heart be in her arms.* But until in His perfect timing He puts a baby in your arms, you can love and pray for the children with whom you come into contact. You can lavish upon them the loving concern that you hope others will lavish upon your children. And you can pray for your yet-unborn child and for every aspect of his or her life.

Prayer's Reach

You can reach into the future through prayer this very day. You can sit in your living room or on the airplane or in the doctor's office and impact the world for generations to come. Consider this: As you pray for generations yet unborn, maybe one of those descendants will take the gospel to a previously unreached corner of the world, so that a people walking in darkness will see a great light, and a light will dawn on those walking in the shadow of death. Your life can impact a people of whom you have never heard, and you can be instrumental in bringing forth generations of believers from a nation you may never see.

It is beyond our imaginations what prayer can effect in the earth. When God's name and His renown are the desire of our heart (Isaiah 26:8), our prayers for our children, grandchildren, and descendants can be the catalyst that will cause His fame to spread to all the corners of the earth.

"Let this be written for a future generation,
that a people not yet created may praise the LORD."

—Psalm 102:18

CHAPTER ONE

A Spiritual Trust Fund

*Prayer puts spiritual riches on deposit
for future generations.*

Store up for yourselves treasures in heaven.
—Matthew 6:20

A Spiritual Trust Fund

Sherry grew up in a non-Christian family. Both parents were alcoholics. Neither they nor her two siblings had any interest in spiritual matters. Yet Sherry as a seven-year-old decided she would like to go to church. Having heard one of her friends talk about it, she asked that friend if she could go with her. From the time she was seven until she could drive herself, Sherry made arrangements to have rides to church every Sunday.

She had no encouragement from home. If she overslept, there was no one to wake her up. She often wondered why she had such an interest in spiritual matters. Where did it come from? At college she met and became engaged to a wonderful Christian man. The first time he took her home to meet his family, her future mother-in-law threw her arms around her and said, "I have been praying for you since before you were born!"

Allana describes her upbringing like this: "I didn't know any Christians. My parents thought people who believed in Jesus were all illiterate. As far as I know, until I reached the fifth grade I had never spoken to a Christian." During her fifth-grade year, a classmate invited her to church.

Allana continued to attend church and after a few years, much to her family's dismay, made a profession of faith in Christ. She grew up, married a Christian man, and had children. Both her parents eventually came to know the Lord. She returned to her hometown for her fifteenth high school reunion. As she was walking through a grocery store, she encountered her fifth-grade teacher. Allana began to share with her the details of her life—whom she had married, where she lived, how many children she had. Finally Allana said, "You were such a wonderful teacher!" The woman replied, "Oh, honey, I don't know how good a teacher I was, but I did pray for each one of my students by name, every day."

Wendy's mother took her to Sunday school and church, but her father did not attend. One Sunday her mother could not take her, so her father dropped her off. That Sunday, at the age of seven,

Wendy invited Jesus into her life. The children's church leader asked her to stay afterward to talk further. When her father came to pick her up, he patiently waited, then listened carefully as she told him about her decision. Three years later, her father committed his life to Christ.

Years later, Wendy was looking through a water-stained pasteboard box full of faded family photographs. She came across a brittle piece of lined paper. The writing on it was faint, but she could make out the words of a handwritten prayer penned by her father's grandmother. "This day, July 10, 1912, I hereby sign and give my son Robert over to the Lord, for the Lord to redeem his soul from sin and make him an earnest Christian." Wendy had found what she now calls "a footprint of faith in a family that had seemed singularly godless." Wendy discovered she had inherited a legacy of prayer from a great-grandmother she had never met.

I have had the privilege of growing up in a family of faithful believers and ardent intercessors. "The boundary lines have fallen for me in pleasant places; surely I have a delightful inheritance" (Psalm 16:6). My great-grandmother, Susan Mynatte Medearis, had eleven children, the youngest of whom was my grandmother, Cleta

Belle Kennedy. If ever you visit the Smithsonian's Museum of American Art, you may see a painting entitled "Godly Susan," by the late Roger Medearis. Godly Susan is my great-grandmother, painted by her grandson.

Susan Medearis was not a woman of wealth. She was not well educated. But Susan Medearis was a woman of prayer. My father, her grandson, remembers that in her last years she spent a few months in each of her children's homes as her children helped care for her. My father recalls that during his childhood her visits were occasions of joy, not dreaded as duty. In fact, she personally led my father to the Lord during one of her visits in his home.

One of her sons, my great-uncle Thomas Whittier Medearis, had a lifetime of distinguished ministry, and is remembered as a man of great integrity and leadership. In remarks Uncle Tom made at a Medearis family reunion, he said, "Never a day passes that I do not pray for every one of my children and their families by name. And then I pray for my living sisters and sisters-in-law, and then for the children of all my brothers and sisters, and their children. I want more than I can say for the Medearis family to present a solid phalanx, always, in the army of the Lord."

Jesus prayed for the future generations of His descendants—those who would be born again by His Spirit. "My prayer is not for them alone. I pray also for those who will believe in me through their message" (John 17:20). Clearly Jesus knew that the prayer He prayed on that day would reach into the future to impact the lives of His followers until the end of time.

> God shapes the world by prayer. Prayers are deathless. The lips that uttered them may be closed in death, the heart that felt them may have ceased to beat, but the prayers live before God, and God's heart is set on them, and prayers outlive the lives of those who uttered them; outlive a generation, outlive an age, outlive a world.
>
> —E. M. Bounds

Prayers Are Deathless

Most often the shorthand definition for prayer is "conversation with God." It *is* that, but it is much more. I say this in nearly every book I write, but I'm going to say it once again: Prayer is the conduit that brings the power and provision of God into the circumstances of earth. When we pray, we are doing more than speaking words. We are impacting the spiritual realm. We are accessing the power, the plan, the riches of heaven. In the material realm—earth—words are mere puffs of air, here now and then gone. The words we speak in prayer, however, are living and active vehicles of God's power. Our prayers are "stored up" in the spiritual realm, to be released at exactly the ripe moment.

In the book of Revelation, where we are given a glimpse into heaven's throne room, we discover "golden bowls full of incense, which are the prayers of the saints" (Revelation 5:8). Bowls full of prayers. Here's what I imagine as a scene in the throne room: The angels call out, "Bring out another bowl for the Dean boys. This one's full!" I want to fill bowls and bowls and bowls with spiritual riches for my sons and my descendants.

O. Hallesby, author of the classic book *Prayer*, writes,

> The longer you live a life of this kind, the more answers to prayer you will experience. As white snowflakes fall quietly and thickly on a winter's day, answers to prayer will settle down on you at every step you take, even to your dying day. ...This shower of answers to prayer will continue to your dying hour. Nor

will it cease then. And when you pass from
beneath the shower, your dear ones will step
into it. Every prayer and every sigh which you
have uttered for them and their future welfare will, in God's time, descend upon them
as a gentle rain of answers to prayers.

Our family has been a believing and praying family for three generations. The elders have prayed
faithfully for their descendants. During my whole
life I have walked in the prayers of my forebears
and in the answers to these prayers. A quiet rain
drips steadily upon me.

I want my sons to walk in a gentle rain of
answered prayers. I often tell them when they face
decisions or difficulties, "You are walking today in
the answers to generations of prayer."

Prayers Are Limitless

Prayer is not limited to linear time, because God is
not limited to linear time. God speaks of the past,
the present, and the future as one. "Before they
call I will answer; while they are still speaking I will
hear" (Isaiah 65:24). His name is I Am. Always in
the present tense.

The answers to the prayers you pray today will
be answered in the lives of your descendants at the

right time. Those answers will be working in their lives as if you had just prayed them. Your prayers will put spiritual riches on deposit for them. They will have spiritual abundance from which they can make withdrawals as need arises. As they learn to pray, they will be accessing the spiritual riches you have stored up for them.

Moses gave insight into the content of his prayers when he addressed Joshua, who was defending Moses' position as a prophet of God among the people. Moses said to Joshua, "Are you jealous for my sake? I wish that all the LORD's people were prophets and that the LORD would put his spirit on them!" (Numbers 11:29). Many generations later, God answered Moses' prayer for his descendants: "'In the last days,' God says, 'I will pour out my Spirit on all people. Your sons and daughters will prophesy, your young men will see visions, your old men will dream dreams. Even on my servants, both men and women, I will pour out my Spirit in those days, and they will prophesy'" (Acts 2:17–18). The very prayer that God initiated in the heart of Moses, and promised in the book of Joel, was fulfilled in the book of Acts. When the ripe moment arrived, the answer to Moses' heart's desire fell upon his descendants as if he had just prayed it.

My friend Janelle has inherited a legacy of prayer from her incredible mother, Arbara. When Arbara died, Janelle felt called to pick up her mother's intercession assignments, but her mother had prayed faithfully for so many people that Janelle felt overwhelmed. Then the Lord showed her how to do it. In her mind's eye, she gathers them all before her and prays over them. When one needs special prayer, the Lord will impress upon her to single that one out.

Janelle knows that as she prays over them collectively, their names are being spoken, one-by-one, in the spiritual realm. I have picked up this practice. In my mind's eye, now, I gather up my sons and my future daughters-in-law and my descendants and pray over them.

Day by day, hour by hour, I am adding to their spiritual trust fund. All their lives they will have the riches of the spiritual realm available to them.

CHAPTER TWO

Investing in Eternity

*The spiritual trust fund I will leave behind
for future generations begins with my own
walk with God.*

He who fears the Lord has a secure fortress, and for his children it will be a refuge.

—Proverbs 14:26

Investing in Eternity

2

$\mathcal{T}$he spiritual inheritance I will leave behind for future generations begins with my own walk with the Lord. As God is my fortress and my stronghold, part of the inheritance I leave—part of my estate –is my dwelling place. "Lord, you have been our dwelling place throughout all generations" (Psalm 90:1). "But the LORD has become *my* fortress, and my God the rock in whom *I* take refuge" (Psalm 94:22, emphases added). I have a dwelling place that is also a stronghold and fortress.

All that I invest in my personal relationship with the Lord will yield a hundred-fold increase (Mark 4:8), and will provide spiritual shelter for future generations. I am nearly fifty years old, but I still take refuge in my parents' faith. When times are hard, my parents' faith, tested and proven through the years, is a safe place for me to run.

Because I have taken shelter there time and again, I have developed my own faith. They are my faith-mentors.

Now I can build a secure fortress of genuine faith for my own children. The stronghold I am building for my children looks a lot like the one my parents built for me. We have the same Architect and the same Interior Decorator. I am adding my own personal touches to the décor, things that are uniquely mine. As I continue personally to discover new depths of faith, I am building a home place for generations to come. As I invest myself in knowing God, I am creating a secure fortress for my children.

A House of Wisdom

Proverbs 24:3–4 says, "By wisdom a house is built, and through understanding it is established; through knowledge its rooms are filled with rare and beautiful treasures." Wisdom is the material of which your dwelling place is built, understanding is its foundation, and knowledge makes it beautiful and pleasant. "The house of the righteous contains great treasure" (Proverbs 15:6).

As you engage in the spiritual disciplines, you are creating for your descendants a dwelling place that is also a stronghold and a refuge—a fortress. As you come to know God for yourself, through firsthand experience, your descendants will be the beneficiaries. Let's examine the disciplines one by one, and maybe cast them in new forms. I'm asking the Lord to give you a fresh outpouring of His Spirit and a revived passion for seeking His face.

The Word

The written Word, the Bible, is only words on pages bound in a book, *unless* the Living Word Himself speaks it to you. As He breathes life into the words, they become living and active, able to divide soul from spirit (Hebrews 4:12). Jesus is the living, speaking Word. His presence in you imparts life to the Scriptures as you read them. As He speaks His Word to you, the words He speaks are Spirit and Life. The Bible becomes something altogether different.

If you look to the Bible for answers to your deepest needs, you will not find them. But if you look to *Jesus,* you will find the answers to your deepest needs in the Bible. Jesus warns against putting our faith in the Bible rather than in Him: "You diligently study the Scriptures because you think that by them you possess eternal life. These are the Scriptures that testify about me, yet you refuse to come to me to have life" (John 5:39–40). I love the Bible. I treasure it. I delight in it. In the Scriptures I hear the voice of the One I treasure, the One in whom I delight, the One my soul loves. When I open my Bible, this prayer is in my heart: "Show me your face, let me hear your voice; for your voice is sweet, and your face is lovely" (Song of Solomon 2:14).

If you read God's Word as if it were a book of rules or a textbook, or even a book of wisdom, your soul will not be fed. If you come to His Word as the meeting place between your heart and His, "[your] soul will be satisfied as with the richest of foods" (Psalm 63:5).

> Help me, O God,
> To measure all the words in the Scriptures,
> but to treasure them only as they lead to You.
> May the words be stepping-stones in finding You,
> and if I am to get lost at all in the search,
> may it not be down a theological rabbit trail,
> or in some briar patch of controversy.
> If I am to get lost at all,
> grant that it be in Your arms.
> Help me love You the way Mary did.

And may something of the spilling passion of
her devotion spill into me.
—from *Windows of the Soul,* by Ken Gire

God is your dwelling place and your fortress. God
is your home and your protection. As you meet
Him in His Word—as His Word reveals depths of
truth, and as the power of His living voice changes
you—your life is filled with rare and beautiful treasures that you will pass along to future generations.

"He will be the sure foundation for your
times,
a rich store of salvation and wisdom
and knowledge;
the fear of the LORD is the key to this
treasure."
—Isaiah 33:6

Prayer

Prayer is a life. Prayer flows through you without
ceasing, sometimes in the foreground, sometimes
in the background. In my book *Live a Praying Life:
Open Your Life to God's Power and Provision,* I go into
great depth about living prayer.

But a life of prayer is undergirded and nurtured
through the discipline of focused times of prayer.

You must intentionally schedule daily periods of time for undistracted interaction with God. Your time in the Scripture and in prayer will be the same: As you seek Him in His Word, He is speaking to you and awakening thoughts in you. As you respond to those thoughts, prayer is taking place.

As you become deliberate about setting aside time for prayer, don't force yourself into someone else's mold. You are a unique design, and God will interact with you in ways that fit your personality. Some personalities love structure, others are inhibited by too much structure. Don't gauge your prayer time by measuring it against someone else's. Your daily time of focused prayer shouldn't feel like duty, but delight. The only duty you have during that time is to delight yourself in Him.

As you take time daily for uninterrupted delight in God, you fill your life with treasures that will last throughout the generations. You discover more of Jesus, "in whom are hidden all the treasures of wisdom and knowledge" (Colossians 2:3).

Fasting

Jesus gave specific instructions for how to fast. Clearly He expects His followers to incorporate fasting in the spiritual disciplines. Don't become legalistic about fasting, but do be receptive to it when the Spirit calls you into a time of fasting.

"When you fast, do not look somber as the hypocrites do, for they disfigure their faces to show men they are fasting. I tell you the truth, they have received their reward in full. But when you fast, put oil on your head and wash your face, so that it will not be obvious to men that you are fasting, but only to your Father, who is unseen; and your Father, who sees what is done in secret, will reward you."
—Matthew 6:16–18

Jesus expected His disciples to fast. "How can the guests of the bridegroom mourn while he is with them? The time will come when the bridegroom will be taken from them; then *they will fast*" (Matthew 9:15, emphasis added).

Jesus Himself often fasted as part of His ongoing life of prayer. Throughout history, men and women whose lives have displayed the power and provision of God made fasting part of their spiritual arsenal. Andrew Murray, in his book *With Christ in the School of Prayer,* says, "Faith needs a life of prayer in which to grow and keep strong. ...Prayer needs fasting for its full and perfect development." My friend, if you are craving the fullness of His power, you cannot ignore the discipline of fasting.

What is the purpose of a fast? To fast is to abstain from food. The literal meaning of the Hebrew word for *fast* is "to cover the mouth." You might also abstain from other activities during a fast. How would refusing food make a difference in prayer? What could possibly be the link between the two?

Food sustains and nourishes your physical body. When we eat food, we literally take the earth and make it part of us. I am convinced that God designed our bodies to be nourished and fueled in this way so that we might have a picture of true nourishment—the eternal nourishment of our spirits. "It is written: 'Man does not live on bread alone, but on every word that comes from the mouth of God' " (Matthew 4:4).

God has represented His Word as food that nourishes our spiritual life in the same way that physical food nourishes our physical life. Read Psalm 119:103–104, Jeremiah 15:16, and Ezekiel 3:1–4. Just as food strengthens and maintains our bodies, the Word of God nourishes, fuels, and strengthens our spirits.

During a fast, you are deliberately letting go of that which binds you to this physical world—

food—in order to receive all your sustenance from the spiritual world. In fasting, you determine that for a period of time you will deny your physical cravings in order to focus on your spiritual cravings. You will allow your spiritual hunger to become stronger and more focused. You will feed your spirit with the same enthusiasm with which you feed your body. During a fast, spiritual hunger takes priority over physical hunger. O. Hallesby says, "Fasting loosens the ties which bind us to this world of material things and our surroundings as a whole, that we may concentrate all our spiritual powers upon the unseen and eternal."

Fasting is not a way to influence, impress, or manipulate God. Fasting does not prove anything to God. It doesn't show Him whether or not you are serious. He knows your heart better than you do. "Nothing in all creation is hidden from God's sight. Everything is uncovered and laid bare before the eyes of him to whom we must give account" (Hebrews 4:13). A fast is not a hunger strike designed to convince God to release what He has, up to now, held back. Fasting is not a last-ditch effort to get through to God. Instead, it sharpens our spiritual senses so that God can get through to us.

As you learn to fast when God calls you to, you are feasting on the true Bread, "the living bread that came down from heaven" (John 6:51). You are filling your life with precious and valuable furnishings. You are furnishing your life with His powerful words, letting them dwell richly in you (Colossians 3:16). "I have treasured the words of his mouth more than my daily bread" (Job 23:12).

Giving

God has led me to look into why He chooses to finance His work and meet the needs of His children through the gifts of His people. Primarily, He has shown me that He allows His people to give because that obedience releases His abundance (Luke 6:38).

This truth may be found throughout Scripture. I have paid particular attention to His wonderful promise to provide for all our needs through His riches in Christ Jesus (Philippians 4:19). Look at the thoughts that lead up to that promise:

"I rejoice greatly in the Lord that at last you have renewed your concern for me. Indeed, you have been concerned, but you had no opportunity to show it. I am not saying this because I am in need,

for I have learned to be content whatever the circumstances. I know what it is to be in need, and I know what it is to have plenty. I have learned the secret of being content in any and every situation, whether well fed or hungry, whether living in plenty or in want. I can do everything through him who gives me strength."
—Philippians 4:10–13

The Philippians are not the source of Paul's supply. God is the source of his supply. Paul is not dependent upon the gifts of the Philippians; but they need an opportunity to show their commitment in tangible ways. Paul is looking to His Father for all of his needs.

"Yet it was good of you to share in my troubles. Moreover, as you Philippians know, in the early days of your acquaintance with the gospel, when I set out from Macedonia, not one church shared with me in the matter of giving and receiving, except you only; for even when I was in Thessalonica, you sent me aid again and again when I was in need. Not that I am looking for a gift, but I am looking for what may be credited to your account."
—Philippians 4:14–17

Paul is doing the Philippians a favor by allowing them to give!

"I have received full payment and even more; I am amply supplied, now that I have received from Epaphroditus the gifts you sent. They are a fragrant offering, an acceptable sacrifice, pleasing to God."
—Philippians 4:18

God sees our gifts as "a fragrant offering, an acceptable sacrifice, well-pleasing to God." Giving is worship!

"And my God will meet all your needs according to his glorious riches in Christ Jesus."
—Philippians 4:19

Giving activates the wonderful promise that God will supply all your needs.

"To our God and Father be glory for ever and ever. Amen."
—Philippians 4:20

The ultimate result of our giving is that God is glorified.

We are the Body of Christ. When I give, I am pouring out costly ointment, anointing the body of Jesus as an act of love and worship to Him. My prayer is that God will give you many opportunities to give—and give—and give some more, and that you will find an even fuller measure of His overflowing joy. As you engage in the spiritual discipline of giving, you are discovering that "where your treasure is, there your heart will be also" (Luke 12:34). You are allowing God to fill your heart with the kind of treasure that will never diminish in value.

Fellowship with Other Believers

Jesus prayed, "May they be brought to complete unity to let the world know that you sent me and have loved them even as you have loved me" (John 17:23). He calls the church His body, and makes it clear that we cannot reach maturity outside the body of Christ. The fullness of Christ is in His body.

"And God placed all things under his feet and appointed him to be head over everything for the church, which is his body, the fullness of him who fills everything in every way. ...until we all reach

unity in the faith and in the knowledge of the Son of God and become mature, attaining to the whole measure of the fullness of Christ."
—Ephesians 1:22–23, 4:13

Our unity is in Him. Each part of the body has a different function, but the same blood flows through them all. What makes us—the different parts of His body—one? The same Life flows through us all. "There is one body and one Spirit—just as you were called to one hope when you were called—one Lord, one faith, one baptism; one God and Father of all, who is over all and through all and in all" (Ephesians 4:4–6). It is in the context of the body that we find our fullness and reach maturity.

As you fellowship with other believers and bring your life into unity with them, you are filling your life with the beauty of Jesus. You are building a dwelling place and fortress for future generations.

Spiritual Treasures

"He who fears the Lord has a secure fortress, and *for his children* it will be a refuge" (Proverbs 14:26, emphasis added). As you seek the Lord yourself, you are laying up treasures for future generations. As you invest in your own walk with the Lord, you are investing in eternity.

When I was a little girl, my mother's grandmother, my great-grandmother, had a beautiful collection of cut crystal in her home. How I loved it! I would admire it for long periods every time I was in her home. She would tell me the history of each piece—where she got it, who gave it to her, or the occasion it represented. The crystal grew in value to me because of her history. My mother would tell me how much she also loved the crystal when she was a little girl my age. As the crystal became, in my mind, part of my mother's history as well, it took on still more value to me.

After the death of "Big Grandma," as we called her, the crystal came to my mother, and for many years was part of my daily experience. Now my mother has given it to me. I see it nearly every day, and it always reminds me of when I would sit on my great-grandmother's lap. I remember how she looked and smelled, and how her voice sounded.

To me, each piece is a rare and beautiful treasure. Although there are likely other pieces that look like these, those other pieces don't have my great-grandmother's history, my mother's history, and my history in them.

Some day I will give the pieces to my future daughters-in-law. But I will also pass on to them the history of each piece. I will do my best to help them know my great-grandmother. Maybe I'll even get to tell my grandchildren. The special value of the pieces, I hope, will be passed on and on. They will increase in value—not monetary value, but true value—with each generation because they will have more and more history.

So it is with the riches you are building into your life. As you take them out and show them to your children and your grandchildren and your great-grandchildren, they will learn to love and value them. They will say to themselves, "Someday I want that treasure in my life." As the Lord teaches them as He has taught you, the wisdom, understanding, and insight they gain in their walk will have even more value because it echoes your history with the Lord.

My dad has always loved the Scripture. My childhood memories are peppered with scenes of Daddy as he sat reading the Bible privately, or as he read to us at family devotionals, or as he reclined across the foot of our beds at night and led us to memorize verses and passages of Scripture. When I read from the King James Version, I hear my father's voice. He made me love the Word of God.

My mother has always been excited about prayer. My earliest memories include her prayer groups and her excitement in telling us about great prayer adventures. She made me crave prayer.

I am convinced that certain flesh-strongholds and sin-patterns are also passed down through generations. When a flesh-stronghold runs through generations, it seems to increase its hold in each generation. But when we learn to make God our stronghold, we can pass that divine stronghold along to future generations.

Each person will come to a saving relationship with the Father through the Son on his or her own. Our descendants will not inherit salvation. Each person will get to know God for himself or herself. Our descendants will not be able to live on secondhand information about God. But the tendency will be there. The passion and the inclination will be there. And then, as God reveals Himself, there will be a certain recognition, and the treasures He gives them will have a familiar feel to them.

"'My Spirit, who is on you, and my words that I have put in your mouth will not depart from your mouth, or from the mouths of your children, or

from the mouths of their descendants from this time on and forever,' says the LORD."
—Isaiah 59:21

CHAPTER THREE

Generation to Generation

*God defines Himself to the new generation
in terms of the previous generations.*

One generation will commend your works to another; they will tell of your mighty acts.

—Psalm 145:4

Generation to Generation

God defines Himself to one generation in terms of the previous generation. When God came to Moses in a burning bush, Moses asked God who he should say had sent him. The reply came: "Say to the Israelites, 'The LORD, the God of your fathers—the God of Abraham, the God of Isaac and the God of Jacob—has sent me to you.' This is my name forever, the name by which I am to be remembered from generation to generation" (Exodus 3:15). Would that name have meant anything to a person who did not know about Abraham, or Isaac, or Jacob?

When God speaks to my sons, calling them to take faith risks in obedience to Him, I want Him to be able to say, "I am the God of your parents. I am the God of Wayne and Jennifer." And I want them to be able to respond, "I've seen You work all my life. I've experienced Your faithfulness. I know that I can trust You."

We need to mentor our children in prayer and faith. We have to make them part of our journey of discovery. We have to quit shielding them from our own struggles—the ones they can handle within the context of their age and maturity level. I used to think that I should let my children see only my faith, never my fear or my doubt or my struggle. Later I realized that they thought I never had struggles or doubts. I have found it more to their advantage to let them see the whole process.

I don't mean that you should burden your children with struggles they are too young to comprehend. But as they mature, let them see *inside* the life of faith. Let them have an up-close view of the whole experience of living by the principles of faith.

When God said to Moses, "I am the God of Abraham and the God of Jacob and the God of Isaac," He was pointing to three aspects of His work in our lives. We need to introduce all three of these aspects to our children through our own walk with the Lord. As we come to know God more and more intimately—all aspects of His character and His power—our children will see Him working in our lives and will look for His work in their own lives.

You must be able to discern God's work in your own life before you can teach it to your children.

"Only be careful, and watch yourselves closely so that you do not forget the things your eyes have seen or let them slip from your heart as long as you live. Teach them to your children and to their children after them."
—Deuteronomy 4:9

The God of Abraham

Abraham represents the walk of faith. Scripture records three seasons in the life of Abraham— each inaugurated by an act of faith. The book of Hebrews records them:

"*By faith* Abraham, when called to go to a place he would later receive as his inheritance, obeyed and went, even though he did not know where he was going."
—Hebrews 11:8, emphasis added

"*By faith* Abraham, even though he was past age— and Sarah herself was barren—was enabled to become a father because he considered him faithful who had made the promise."
—Hebrews 11:11, emphasis added

"By faith Abraham, when God tested him, offered Isaac as a sacrifice. He who had received the promises was about to sacrifice his one and only son, even though God had said to him, 'It is through Isaac that your offspring will be reckoned.'"
—Hebrews 11:17–18, emphasis added

Abraham left his home, he became a father to Isaac, and he offered Isaac on the altar. Each of these events, recognized in Scripture to be acts of faith, was initiated by God. Each act of faith was a direct response to God's voice. The God of Abraham is faithful to His promises. He can be trusted no matter how the circumstances may appear. He is the One you can trust, even when you don't understand.

Are you living in such intimacy with the God of Abraham that you hear His voice? Are you learning to trust Him so fully that you hold firmly to His promises no matter how impossible they may seem? No matter how much your circumstances seem to contradict His promise, do you "consider Him faithful who has made the promise"? Do you know the God of Abraham so well that you are confident that you will never lose anything you lay on His altar? As your descendants learn your history, will they see the God of Abraham?

Right now, the God of Abraham—your God—
has placed you at the crossroads of one of these
three kinds of faith. Has He called on you to take
an action, but you hesitate because you don't
know the step that will follow? You can't see for
sure where that step will lead? Do the one thing
you know, and let the God of Abraham reveal
Himself to you. Let Him lead you to the place He
has in mind. He knows where He's going, so you
don't have to. As He said to Abraham: "Leave your
country, your people and your father's household
and go *to the land I will show you*" (Genesis 12:1,
emphasis added).

Has God planted a promise in you, but the circumstances seem to make its fulfillment impossible? Are you doubting that it was God after all? Yet
in the quiet and intimate moments with Him, the
promise is still alive in your heart. I love these
words that describe Abraham's faith: "Against all
hope, Abraham in hope *believed* and *so became* the
father of many nations, just as it had been said to
him" (Romans 4:18, emphasis added). *Believed and
so became.* Abraham was "fully persuaded that God
had power to do what he had promised" (Romans
4:21). Let the God of Abraham prove Himself true
to His word. You can have outrageous confidence
in the God of Abraham.

Do you know God's heart well enough to trust anything He calls you to do? We will deal with this last faith challenge—to put Isaac on the altar—in the next chapter. But in your walk with God, is He calling you to give Him full possession and absolute control of something or someone who is precious to you? If you know the God of Abraham, you can trust His heart. If you know the God of Abraham, you know you can risk everything on His faithfulness. Obey, and let the God of Abraham show Himself to you.

Your God is the God of Abraham. Respond to Him in faith, and He will say to your descendants: "You know Me. You've seen My power and My faithfulness. You can trust Me. I'm the God of your parents and your grandparents. I'm the God of Abraham."

The God of Isaac

Isaac represents grace. Everything that Isaac owned belonged to him for only one reason: he was Abraham's son. Everything that Abraham accumulated became Isaac's by virtue of his birth. He was born into his father's kingdom, so everything his father owned was his.

Isaac's position had nothing to do with who he was, and everything to do with who his father was. Paul says that Isaac was not born "in the ordinary way," but instead was born "by the power of the Spirit" (Galatians 4:29). When we are born into the kingdom of our Father, we are not born in the ordinary way, either. We are born by the power of the Spirit. "Yet to all who received him, to those who believed in his name, he gave the right to become children of God—children born not of natural descent, nor of human decision or a husband's will, but born of God" (John 1:12–13).

Do you know the God of Isaac? Do you know that everything the Father has belongs to you (John 16:14–15; Galatians 3:29, 4:7)? Are you learning to live as a recipient of the Father's riches? Are you building a legacy of peace and confidence in your Father? Are you putting out the treasures your Father has given you for all to see? Are you teaching your descendants to trust the God of Isaac?

Respond to God's grace, and He will be able to say to your descendants: "You know Me. I'm the God of your parents—the God who provided for their every need and lavished upon them the gifts of the spiritual realm. I am the God of Isaac."

The God of Jacob

Jacob represents sanctification. Jacob was a dishonest, scheming, crafty, manipulative person. He represents our flesh—those parts of our lives where we depend on ourselves rather than the power of God. The God of Jacob is working in our lives to wrestle our flesh into submission so that the power of the Spirit can operate freely in us.

This aspect of God's work, I think, is the most easily observed. As your children gain maturity, they can see whether you are truly allowing the Spirit to overcome your flesh and nail it to the cross, or whether you are simply disguising your flesh and putting on a good show for other people. In our homes, we are seen for who we are. Our flesh is not hidden.

In my book *He Restores My Soul*, I wrote about crucifixion of the flesh and the resurrection power that results. I identified "crucifixion moments"—junctures at which our flesh is brought to the surface and we have a choice to make. We can act in our old flesh-pattern, strengthening it; or we can yield that flesh to its death sentence. Denise Glenn calls such moments of choice "when the cross crosses your life" (*MotherWise: Freedom for Mothers*). Our lives are full of such moments—some monumental, some little. Our families see many of them, but not all of them.

The way in which I deal with a crucifixion moment is the proof of my heart. If I let my children in on the crucifixion process, revealing my own weaknesses and struggles, they get a bird's-eye view of how it works. If my life authenticates my message, the message grows in value to them. Then, when the cross crosses their lives, they have a model of how to yield to the crucifixion. But they also have seen the resurrection that follows. They are far more equipped to be ready to endure the pain of a crucifixion moment for the joy of resurrection power. When God says, "I am the God of Jacob," they can say, "I want all of You. I want You to wrestle my flesh into submission, because I've seen what resurrection looks like."

If I don't let my children in on the crucifixion, they won't see the resurrection. If I don't let them in on the battle, they won't see the victory. If I don't let them in on the need, they won't see the supply. I find that if I am open with them, they are likely to be open with me. Now that they are almost adults, they often let me in on their crucifixion moments, and I have the privilege of praying them through those and seeing them develop into men after God's own heart. I want them to know the God of Jacob.

Recording History

Of course, I don't tell my children every thought
that crosses my mind. I don't bombard them day
and night with stories of my faith walk and my
prayer odyssey, much as I'd like to! For that I keep
a journal. My journal is a record of God's work in
my life and I hope it stands as a testimony to the
power and grace and love of God for many generations.

"I will utter hidden things, things from
of old—
what we have heard and known,
what our fathers have told us.
We will not hide them from their
children;
we will tell the next generation
the praiseworthy deeds of the Lord,
his power, and the wonders he has done.
He decreed statutes for Jacob
and established the law in Israel,
which he commanded our forefathers
to teach their children,
so the next generation would know them,
even the children yet to be born,
and they in turn would tell their
children.

Then they would put their trust in God
and would not forget his deeds
but would keep his commands."
—Psalm 78:2–7

There are many ways to record your history with
God besides the traditional way of journaling. My
dad writes a monthly letter to friends and family. It
is a collection of his observations and thoughts,
newsy incidents, stories, jokes, and such. He writes
on it all month long, kind of like a journal. It
keeps us all in touch with each other and also provides a history. When those of us on his mailing list
meet from time to time, we'll often say, "I read
about you recently in The Letter." People share
The Letter with their friends and some have even
requested to be added to the mailing list. I save all
the letters and they have given me many glimpses
into my dad's heart. Because of The Letter, we can
go back and read things such as detailed accounts
of each of his grandchildren's professions of faith.

E-mail is a wonderful invention. By saving e-
mails between me, my husband, and our sons, I
preserve a faith history.

I also have a journal for each of my three sons.
I write in each journal things that are significant
for that individual child. I don't write in them

much. My tradition is to write in them on their birthdays, reflecting on the year and writing my prayer for them for that year. Sometimes I have written in them on times other than their birthdays, but not often. They've never seen these journals. I don't know when I'll give them their journals, but someday I will.

Your Bible becomes a journal and a faith history as you write personal notes in it. A Bible becomes an irreplaceable treasure, a rare and priceless possession, when it has the hand-written thoughts of an ancestor.

My great-uncle, whom I previously mentioned—Tom Medearis, Godly Susan's son—wrote his memories of his father. He called it "Following Pa to the Promised Land." I love it, and can barely keep myself from quoting passages to you. But I realize that you will not find it nearly as fascinating as I do. In it I meet a great-grandfather I never knew. I see in him a certain sense of humor, a certain way of viewing life, that I recognize in my dad, and in myself, and in my sons. In Uncle Tom's writing style I see shadows of my own. It reminds me that part of God's design for my life is that I come from a certain line of ancestors. What He did in their lives is passed down to me and then to my sons and, someday, to my grandchildren. "But the plans of the Lord stand firm forever, the purposes of his heart through all generations" (Psalm 33:11). I am part of an ongoing work of God, as are my children and my descendants.

I want to find ways to leave for my descendants a record of their legacy. "Even when I am old and gray, do not forsake me, O God, till I declare your power to the next generation, your might to all who are to come" (Psalm 71:18). I want them to know the God of Abraham, the God of Isaac, and the God of Jacob.

CHAPTER FOUR

Pray in the Spirit

In order to pray for future generations, we must die to our flesh connections with them and remain alive to the spiritual promise in them. Our flesh is protective and possessive. We are all called to place our children and our descendants on the altar, abandoning them to God's purpose and plan for their lives.

Flesh gives birth to flesh, but the Spirit gives birth to spirit.

—John 3:6–7

The Spirit gives life; the flesh counts for nothing.

—John 6:63

Pray in the Spirit

*I*n praying for our children, our grandchildren, and our descendants, we must learn to pray in the Spirit and not in the flesh. Our mother-flesh and our father-flesh is protective and possessive. The love we have for our children, in its flesh form, would like to control their lives and keep them from any pain, disappointment, or discouragement. Our flesh wants to rescue them and shield them and run interference for them. Our flesh will pray, "Don't let anything bad happen." To which the Lord will say, "I need to allow disappointment, pain, and failure so that I can give him the treasures of darkness and the riches stored in secret places." If we pray for our children from our flesh rather than the Spirit, we may think that God is not listening when our children *do* have difficulties.

As we pray for our children, we must die to our flesh connection with them and remain alive to the spiritual promise in them. Consider the story of Abraham, when God called on him to place Isaac on the altar.

On the Altar

To see this principle, we need to look at the account in the book of Genesis and the commentary on the story in the book of Hebrews.

The story begins, "God tested Abraham. He said to him, 'Abraham!' 'Here I am,' he replied. Then God said, 'Take your son, your only son, Isaac, whom you love, and go to the region of Moriah. Sacrifice him there as a burnt offering on one of the mountains I will tell you about.' Early the next morning Abraham got up and saddled his donkey" (Genesis 22:1–3).

God tested Abraham. The word *test* is better translated "proved." When God tests, He is not trying to discover what is inside us. He knows what is inside us. He is *proving* what is inside us. He is bringing what is inside to the outside. Don't think of this as a "trick" on God's part. He is not trying to trip Abraham up; He is proving to Abraham what God knows is in him. In the book of

Hebrews, we have an explanation of God's dealing
with Abraham.

"By faith Abraham, when God tested him, offered
Isaac as a sacrifice. He who had received the
promises was about to sacrifice his one and only
son, even though God had said to him, "It is
through Isaac that your offspring will be reckoned." Abraham reasoned that God could raise
the dead, and figuratively speaking, he did receive
Isaac back from death."
—Hebrews 11:17–19

You remember the story. Just as Abraham was
about to plunge the knife into Isaac, an angel of
the Lord stopped him. Yet the writer of Hebrews
says, "Abraham offered Isaac." He uses a verb
tense that indicates a completed action. In the
Amplified Bible it is translated: "Abraham completed the offering of Isaac." Didn't Abraham stop
short of completing the offering? But the Bible
says that he offered Isaac, completing the sacrifice.
When did Abraham complete the offering?

Go back to the account in Genesis. In the
abbreviated version, God called Abraham to offer
Isaac as a sacrifice, and the next morning Abraham got up and saddled his donkey for the trip.

But between God's call and Abraham's obedience lay a long, dark night of struggle. You and I are left to imagine how intense that struggle must have been. We can guess at the agony through which Abraham passed. Our hearts hear Abraham crying out something like this: "If You would, let this cup pass from me!" And before the morning broke, we hear him just as clearly say, "Nevertheless, not my will, but Yours be done." It was in that dark night that Abraham completed the offering of Isaac. It was there that God received what He was asking for. How do I know that?

One of the layers of meaning in this account is that it is a picture of the crucifixion. Follow the timeline with me. Abraham got up, saddled his donkey, and set out for the place God would show Him (Genesis 22:2). He traveled for *three days* (Genesis 22:4), then took Isaac to the top of the mountain and prepared to sacrifice him on the altar. Instead of killing Isaac, God stopped him and Abraham received Isaac back in a resurrection: "and figuratively speaking, he did receive Isaac back from death" (Hebrews 11:19). If Abraham traveled for three days and on the third day received Isaac back in a type of resurrection, then when did Isaac die? The sacrifice was completed on the long, agonizing night that brought about

Abraham's yielded obedience. Three days later, Abraham received Isaac back in a resurrection.

Abraham's Sacrifice

God considered the sacrifice to be completed. God got what He was after. What was God wanting from Abraham? What was the sacrifice?

Abraham was connected to Isaac in two ways: First, Isaac was the son of his flesh. He was to Abraham "your son, your only son, Isaac, whom you love" (Genesis 22:2). You can imagine how very strong that connection was. After having waited and yearned for this son until all rational hope was gone and his and Sarah's bodies were long past childbearing years, at last Isaac was born. As his son, in the days of Abraham, Isaac was his property. He had the right to do with him as he chose. You know that every choice Abraham made concerning Isaac was made out of an overflow of love.

Abraham was connected to Isaac in another way. Isaac was also the child of promise, born by the power of the Spirit (Galatians 4:28–29). It was through Isaac that all of the promise of God—that which had defined Abraham's entire adult life— was to be realized. "He who had received the promises was about to sacrifice his one and only son, *even though God had said* to him, 'It is through

Isaac that your offspring will be reckoned'"
(Hebrews 11:17–19, emphasis added). Abraham
was connected to Isaac spiritually. Isaac was to
Abraham both the child of his flesh and the child
of the promise.

On the night that Abraham completed the
offering, Isaac did not die to Abraham, but Abraham died to his flesh connection with Isaac. He let
his father-flesh die. He relinquished ownership.
That was the night he laid Isaac on the altar.

In requiring Abraham to die to his flesh connection, God did not require Abraham to die to
the spiritual promise. Abraham, I believe, was
more alive than ever to the promise in Isaac. As he
reached the place of the sacrifice, "he said to his
servants, 'Stay here with the donkey while I and
the boy go over there. *We will worship* and then *we
will come back to you*' (Genesis 22:5, emphases
added). The writer of Hebrews says, "Abraham reasoned that God could raise the dead, and figuratively speaking, he did receive Isaac back from
death" (Hebrews 11:19). By the time he had
become fully yielded to the voice of God, by the
time he had dealt the death-blow to his own flesh,
he had reached a new level of faith in God. He was
absolutely certain that, no matter what path the
promise took, the promise of God would not fail.

Abraham had already seen God bring life out of death. "Against all hope, Abraham in hope believed and so became the father of many nations, just as it had been said to him, 'So shall your offspring be.' Without weakening in his faith, he faced the fact that *his body was as good as dead*—since he was about a hundred years old—and that *Sarah's womb was also dead.* Yet he did not waver through unbelief regarding the promise of God, but was strengthened in his faith and gave glory to God, being fully persuaded that God had power to do what he had promised" (Romans 4:18–21, emphases added). From Abraham's dead loins and Sarah's dead womb, Isaac was born. Isaac *was* a resurrection.

Your Altar

God is calling you with the same call Abraham heard. "Take your son, your daughter, your grandson, your granddaughter, and place him or her on My altar. Relinquish ownership. Die to your flesh connection, but remain alive to My promise. Your third day will come. You will look at this one and say, 'Here is a resurrection.' "

Some of you are praying for children and grandchildren who are not saved or who are living in rebellion against God. Maybe you have been praying long enough that you are having a hard time holding on to hope. If you are the grandparent, then your pain is doubled because you are also feeling your child's pain. May the God of Abraham place His strong and loving arms around you right this minute as He assures you that He is the One "who gives life to the dead and calls into being that which does not exist" (Romans 4:17 NASB). He is the One who has the power to do what He has promised (Romans 4:21).

My dear friend, let me talk to you gently for a moment about the flesh that must go on the altar. Flesh doesn't like to die, and will put up quite a fight. Flesh will justify itself and argue for its life. So listen to the God of Abraham, not to your flesh.

I know that your primary concern is for your child and his or her walk with the Lord. But there may be certain elements of flesh mixed with that concern. Don't feel condemned or scolded. God's purpose is just to show you the "dead weight" you are carrying around that you could let go.

Do you see any pride involved? Is part of your struggle that you are embarrassed? Do you wonder, just a little bit, if people might think you are a bad parent? As a teenager, I was not easy to deal with. I was arrogant and rebellious. My mother and I battled nonstop for several years. But my mother is a woman genuinely committed to God, and she reports a turning point in her dealing with me. One day, when we were involved in yet another argument over whether I had to go to church, I said to her, "It's just your pride. You just can't stand it that one of Audrey Kennedy's kids wouldn't be in church!" (How's that for "attitude"?) Let me tell you the truth: I didn't even mean it. Really, I had great respect for my mother, and would have been shocked to know that her pride entered into it at all. It was just a good weapon, one I could aim for a sure hit.

But Mom says that the truth of my words hit her. It caught her by surprise, and she had to confess that there was certainly an element of pride in her distress over me. She had to let that element of pride die on the altar. In the ensuing days, she prayed over me as I went out the door. The essence of her prayer was, in her words, "Make Jennifer into the daughter she should be."

But the Lord spoke clearly to her and said, "Stop praying for Jennifer and start praying for yourself. Ask Me to make you into the mother Jennifer needs." The focus of our relationship changed. Within days, she says, our relationship began to smooth out. She quit trying to fix me and began to just allow God to work in her. She quit being con-

cerned about what other people might think. I did
not know about all this at the time, but I do know
that my senior year was the first harmonious year we
had in some time, and I, too, began to change. All
because she was willing to recognize and relinquish
the pride that was mixed with her desire for me to
live in right relationship with the Father.

Is there some element of a desire to be in control mixed with your concern for your child? Are
you frustrated that you can't make things happen
the way you want them to? Might you need to take
your flesh that needs to be in control and put it on
the altar? My friend Denise Glenn, founder of
MotherWise, tells of a time when God confronted
her about her desire to control her oldest daughter Danielle.

I don't have room here to quote the whole
story, but here is a synopsis. You'll find the complete story in her book *MotherWise: Freedom for
Mothers.*

Danielle is a member of the popular Christian
band, Caedmon's Call. When Danielle was 18 years
old, the band began to tour. Denise struggled with
the fact that Danielle was making choices that
didn't fit Denise's plans.

One night, the Lord wakened Denise from a
dream of a nicely set picnic table. He told her to

go to her kitchen and set the table just as she had seen it in her dream. That done, He said to her, "Unset the table."

"Pick up the spoon," He said. "You've been spoon-feeding Danielle. You've been telling her how much mascara to wear and how to wear her hair and clothes. Stop spoon-feeding her and give her the spoon."

Denise picked up the spoon and set it at Danielle's place.

"Pick up the knife. You've been knifing Danielle in the back. Stop knifing her and give her the knife."

Realizing that indeed she had been angry at Danielle and had been taking it out on her with criticism, Denise picked up the knife and laid it at Danielle's place.

"Now, pick up the fork. Danielle is at a fork in the road. It's not your fork, it's hers. Give her the fork."

At this, Denise began to argue, "Lord, what if she makes the wrong choices? What if she throws away her life?"

"Give her the fork. She is My child and I will deal with her."

With trembling hands, Denise picked up the fork and put it at Danielle's place.

Next, Denise sensed that she was to tuck the napkin under her chin, as you would for a little child.

"You have had the napkin of overprotection on Danielle all her life. You have protected those little white collars from every gravy stain, every mustard blot, every ketchup drip. Now it's time to take off the napkin of overprotection. Let the gravy fall. Let the ketchup drip. I'm a master at spot removal."

Then Denise was led to write on a sticky note: "major, mate, mission"—the three decisions facing Danielle at that moment. She was to stick the note on a plate.

"Give Danielle the plate. Her major, her mate, and her mission are between Danielle and Me. This is not your life, this is hers. Give her the plate."

Tearfully and reverently, Denise laid down the plate.

"Pick up the salt and pepper. What if someone else seasoned your food to suit his or her own taste? That's what you've been doing to Danielle. Let her season her life to her own taste. Give her the salt and pepper."

Then the cup: "You have been pouring out on Danielle the cup of wrath. Give her the cup of kindness."

As God led Denise through letting go, step-by
step, it was a crucifixion for Denise's flesh. Her
flesh died a slow and agonizing death. But today
Danielle and her husband are happily part of
Caedmon's Call and are expecting their second
baby. Danielle and Denise are as close as a mother
and daughter can be.

Your flesh has in it pride, a desire to control,
protectiveness, and a sense of rightful ownership.
Die to those things. Look at them in the clear light
of day. Name them. And die to them.

Die to the flesh, but stay alive to the promise.

Some who read this are not struggling with children who are lost or rebelling. Your children may
have other challenges and difficulties. Be aware of
your flesh's tendency to try to fix things, try to
smooth out every path, try to manipulate situa-
tions to fit your expectations. Don't let your flesh
deceive you. Your prayers for your children will
not shield them from heartache or even from
wrong turns. Your prayers do, however, guarantee
that every problem, every difficulty, every wrong
choice is already factored into God's big picture.
Every struggle will forge in them a deeper faith
and deeper love for the Father. This is what you
want for them. Let God do His work in them. As
He told Denise, He is a master at spot removal.

The children and grandchildren God has entrusted to you do not belong to you. They are His. Jim Elliot wrote the following words in a letter to his parents:

> I do not wonder that you were saddened at the word of my going to South America. ... This is nothing else than what the Lord Jesus warned us of when He told the disciples that they must become so infatuated with the kingdom and following Him that all other allegiances must become as though they were not. And He never excluded the family tie.
>
> In fact, those loves that we regard as closest, He told us must become as hate in comparison with our desires to uphold His cause. Grieve not, then, if your sons seem to desert you, but rejoice, rather, seeing the will of God done gladly. Remember how the Psalmist described children? He said that they were as an heritage from the Lord, and that every man should be happy who had his quiver full of them. And what is a quiver full of but arrows? And what are arrows for but to shoot? So, with the strong arms of prayer, draw the bowstring back and let the arrows fly—all of them, straight at the Enemy's hosts.

—From *Shadow of the Almighty*, by Elisabeth Elliot (New York: Harper & Brothers, 1958) p. 132.

My Resurrection

As I have written this book, I have woven in my own legacy of prayer. Indeed, I am rich beyond measure. My life is filled with rare and beautiful treasures. But I need to make it very clear that even my rich heritage of intercession has not kept me from experiencing heartache and making mistakes. It has, however, ensured that everything I have experienced or will experience is the raw material from which the Lord will form me into a vessel for His honor. To that end I take a deep breath and tell you the story of my resurrection.

Thirty years ago, at the age of nineteen, I found myself pregnant. In the pages of this book, you have met my parents: two people committed to God, leaders in the church and the community. Thirty years ago it was far more shameful for a young, unmarried woman to be pregnant than it is today. I was away at college and shared an apartment with my sister. She broke the news to my parents for me. Never once did I hear or even feel from them accusation: "How could you have done this to us?" I only knew their love. I know they felt anger and hurt and embarrassment, but I only experienced their support.

I knew that I had every possible choice. I could marry, have an abortion, or raise the child as a single mother. But I knew instantly what God was telling me to do, and never once have I second-guessed it. He wanted me to place the child for adoption.

That was the hardest choice of all, but for once in my life my criterion was not what was best or easiest for me, but what was best for another's life.

The story of God's immediate intervention to put all the details into place is a long one, and I won't tell it here. I want you to know, though, that it was during those months—when I was taken out of my whirlwind life and made to sit still—that I began to study the Scriptures and, although I had known them all my life, they came alive to me. I devoured the Word of God. I listened to His voice. God awakened in me the gifts He had given me and created in me a desire to know Him fully.

I had just turned 20 when I gave birth to a little boy. Against the conventional wisdom of the time, I stayed awake and watched his birth. I held him and fed him for the few days we were in the hospital. I handed him to his parents, and my own grief was somewhat diluted by their tears of joy. Child of my womb, child of their hearts. The answer to their prayers lay in their arms, and, strangely, also the answer to my mother's prayers for me. My wounds tell a resurrection story.

Seven years later to the day, I gave birth to my oldest son, Brantley Quin Dean.

"But the pot he was shaping from the clay was marred in his hands; so the potter formed it into another pot, shaping it as seemed best to him."
—Jeremiah 18:4

Altars

My parents have had many altars on which their flesh connections had to die. The generations of intercession have shielded neither them nor us from troubles, but they have meant that those troubles would serve as openings for God's deeper work and would be part of the design of our lives. My only brother died of leukemia at age 17, but his short life, like the loaves and fishes, has had a multiplied impact. My older sister has gone through the grief of infertility, but now we have Hannah Catherine Pederson, our great joy. My younger sister has struggled with dependence on prescription drugs, but now her life is a resurrection. Like Lazarus, the smell of death was on her, but she is alive. Seeing her, no one could deny the power of God.

My dear friend has prayed for her daughters and for their mates all their lives, yet this week her daughter's divorce became final, ending a painful and chaotic marriage. All I can say to her is that the end of the story has not yet been told. Watch and you will see.

Another friend's heart is breaking over a son who seems lost to a homosexual lifestyle. The end of the story has not yet been told.

When the battle is tough, stand firm. When everyone else has left the battlefield, hold your ground. You are an Eleazar.

"Then the men of Israel retreated, but he [Eleazar] stood his ground and struck down the Philistines till his hand grew tired and froze to the sword. The LORD brought about a great victory that day."
—2 Samuel 23:9–10

Like Eleazar, hold so tightly to your sword that it hurts to let go more than it hurts to hang on. Become one with your sword—"the sword of the

Spirit, which is the word of God" (Ephesians 6:17). Has the hand that holds your sword grown tired? Strike one more time. Has everyone else called the situation hopeless? Stand your ground. The Lord will give a great victory.

Don't think that everything will be easy because you have prayed. Prayer will take you into the heart of the battle. You are Shammah.

"When the Philistines banded together at a place where there was a field full of lentils, Israel's troops fled from them. But Shammah took his stand in the middle of the field. He defended it and struck the Philistines down, and the LORD brought about a great victory."
—2 Samuel 23:11–12

Take your stand in the very center of the battle. Your victory is sure.

Pray in the Spirit

Your flesh prays little prayers. God is able to do far more than you can ask or even imagine (Ephesians 3:20). Let the Spirit direct your praying. Wait it out until the end; don't give up in the middle.

Don't flee the battlefield when the warfare is fierce. You are the sure victor.

CHAPTER FIVE

Making Deposits

Scriptural prayers to pray for your descendants.

For no matter how many promises God has made, they are "Yes" in Christ.
—2 Corinthians 1:20

I am watching to see that my word is fulfilled.
—Jeremiah 1:12

Making Deposits 5

*Y*ou already have God's "yes." Every promise He has made He is ready, willing, and able to do. God needs your "yes" in response to Him, so that you may receive what He is offering. "For no matter how many promises God has made, they are 'Yes' in Christ. And so *through him* the 'Amen' is spoken *by us* to the glory of God" (2 Corinthians 1:20, emphases added).

Look at the elements of prayer here: (1) God takes the initiative and makes the promises; (2) the promises are delivered through Christ; (3) we speak the "Amen"—the "so be it," the "it is so," the "yes"; and thus (4) God is glorified, and the truth about God is put on display.

God gives us His promises in order to awaken hope and expectation in us that will cause us to reach out through prayer and receive His gifts. As we pray His Word, we are simply appropriating what He has made available. We are activating His power and provision.

Following are thirty scriptures to pray for your descendants. Gather up your descendants in your mind's eye—though many of them are yet unborn—and pray the Word of God for them. Among those you gather up will also be the spouses of your direct descendants. Imagine how far-reaching your prayers will be!

1. "If you had responded to my rebuke, I would have poured out my heart to you and made my thoughts known to you" (Proverbs 1:23).

Lord, may my descendants respond to Your love, even when it comes in the form of rebuke. Pour out Your heart and cause them to know Your thoughts.

2. "Therefore, I urge you, brothers, in view of God's mercy, to offer your bodies as living sacrifices, holy and pleasing to God—this is your spiritual act of worship. Do not conform any longer to the pattern of this world, but be transformed by the renewing of your mind. Then you will be able to test and approve what God's will is—his good, pleasing and perfect will" (Romans 12:1–2).

I pray that my descendants will always stand in full view of Your mercy—that Your mercy will fill their horizon—and that they will joyfully offer themselves as thank

offerings, a pleasing aroma to You. May they be trans-
formed from the inside and become living proof that Your
will is good, pleasing, and perfect.

3. "The children of your servants will live in your
presence; their descendants will be established
before you" (Psalm 102:28).

May my descendants live in a constant awareness of
Your presence, and may they be firmly established before
You.

4. "All your sons will be taught by the LORD, and
great will be your children's peace" (Isaiah 54:13).

Lord, I pray that You Yourself will be the teacher of
my descendants. Lead them into all truth (John 16:13),
teaching them truth and wisdom in the inner parts
(Psalm 51:6).

5. "Send forth your light and your truth, let them
guide me; let them bring me to your holy mountain, to the place where you dwell. Then will I go
to the altar of God, to God, my joy and my delight.
I will praise you with the harp, O God, my God"
(Psalm 43:3–4).

Let my descendants be guided by Your Light and Your
Truth. May they know Your Son, Jesus, as the Way, the
Truth, and the Light. Lead them into such sweet inti-
macy with You that You are their joy and delight.

6. "Teach me your way, O LORD, and I will walk in your truth; give me an undivided heart, that I may fear your name. I will praise you, O Lord my God, with all my heart; I will glorify your name forever" (Psalm 86:11–12).

Give my descendants an undivided heart. May they love you with their whole hearts, with their whole minds, with their whole souls. Draw them so strongly to You that nothing else can lay claim to even a corner of their hearts.

7. "And this is my prayer: that your love may abound more and more in knowledge and depth of insight, so that you may be able to discern what is best and may be pure and blameless until the day of Christ, filled with the fruit of righteousness that comes through Jesus Christ—to the glory and praise of God" (Philippians 1:9–11).

Lord, grant to my descendants an abundance of true knowledge and deep insight, and enable them to discern the best in every situation. Let their lives be the branches that display your fruit—the righteousness of Christ.

8. "Not only so, but we also rejoice in our sufferings, because we know that suffering produces perseverance; perseverance, character; and character, hope. And hope does not disappoint us, because

God has poured out his love into our hearts by the Holy Spirit, whom he has given us" (Romans 5:3–5).

Lord, give my descendants such wisdom in the things of God that they will see their difficulties and hardships as opportunities for You to develop Christlikeness in them. Complete Your full work in their hearts.

9. "For I will pour water on the thirsty land, and streams on the dry ground; I will pour out my Spirit on your offspring, and my blessing on your descendants. They will spring up like grass in a meadow, like poplar trees by flowing streams" (Isaiah 44:3–5).

May my descendants be drenched in Your Spirit. Create in them such a thirst for You that they long for You like a thirsty land longs for water (Psalm 63:1).

10. "Show me your ways, O LORD, teach me your paths; guide me in your truth and teach me, for you are God my Savior, and my hope is in you all day long" (Psalm 25:4–5).

Lord, teach my descendants Your paths and Your truth, so that they will place all their hope and expectation in You alone.

11. "Then our sons in their youth will be like well-nurtured plants, and our daughters will be like

pillars carved to adorn a palace" (Psalm 144:12).

Even in their youth, may my descendants have a spiritual strength and maturity that is evident to all.

12. "Direct me in the path of your commands, for there I find delight. Turn my heart toward your statutes and not toward selfish gain" (Psalm 119:35–36).

Let my descendants find their delight in Your ways. Keep them from self-centered, self-involved lives, and instead turn their hearts toward You. Give them a passion for You that causes them to honor You in all their ways.

13. "My heart is steadfast, O God" (Psalm 108:1).

Give my descendants steadfast hearts, anchored in You, unshakeable and immovable. May my descendants always present a solid phalanx in the army of the Lord.

14. "Keep me from deceitful ways; be gracious to me through your law. I have chosen the way of truth; I have set my heart on your laws" (Psalm 119:29–30).

Cause my descendants to set their hearts on Your laws and choose Your way. Let deceitfulness of any kind be foreign to them. May Your grace be the centerpiece of their lives.

15. "They will be called oaks of righteousness, a planting of the LORD for the display of his splendor" (Isaiah 61:3).

Let the lives of my descendants be living testimony of who You are.

16. "But they could not stand up against his wisdom or the Spirit by whom he spoke" (Acts 6:10).

Lord, may my descendants be so genuinely full of Your Spirit that You will speak through them.

17. "Commit to the LORD whatever you do, and your plans will succeed" (Proverbs 16:3).

Teach my descendants to commit fully their lives to You—taking every thought captive to the obedience of Jesus Christ (2 Corinthians 10:5)—so that their plans will reflect Your will, "and the will of the LORD will prosper in his hand" (Isaiah 53:10).

18. "May those who fear you rejoice when they see me, for I have put my hope in your word" (Psalm 119:74).

Train my descendants in Your ways, Lord. Teach them early to put their hope in You. Give them experiences that prove that You are true to Your Word. Let them testify, "Your promises have been thoroughly tested, and your servant loves them" (Psalm 119:140).

19. "Direct my footsteps according to your word; let no sin rule over me. Redeem me from the oppression of men, that I may obey your precepts. Make your face shine upon your servant and teach me your decrees" (Psalm 119:133–135).

Set my descendants free from any sinful inclination that may have been passed down through generations. May they live in the freedom that Jesus Christ offers.

20. "I keep asking that the God of our Lord Jesus Christ, the glorious Father, may give you the Spirit of wisdom and revelation, so that you may know him better. I pray also that the eyes of your heart may be enlightened in order that you may know the hope to which he has called you, the riches of his glorious inheritance in the saints, and his incomparably great power for us who believe" (Ephesians 1:17–19).

May my descendants have clear spiritual vision to know and understand Your kingdom. Reveal Yourself to them, that they may know You in Your fullness.

20. "Teach me, O LORD, to follow your decrees; then I will keep them to the end. Give me understanding, and I will keep your law and obey it with all my heart"(Psalm 119:33).

May my descendants have both knowledge and understanding in Your Word.

21. "I have heard that the spirit of the gods is in you and that you have insight, intelligence and outstanding wisdom" (Daniel 5:14–15).

Lord, I pray that my descendants will be like Daniel. May You be so clearly evident in their lives that unbelievers come to them to discover their secret. Grant them insight, intelligence, and wisdom.

22. "Let salvation spring up, let righteousness grow with it" (Isaiah 45:8).

May every one of my descendants come to a saving knowledge of Jesus Christ as his or her Lord and Savior. May their lives be righteous because of You.

23. "May the words of my mouth and the meditation of my heart be pleasing in your sight, O LORD, my Rock and my Redeemer" (Psalm 19:14).

Lord, work mightily in the deep places in the lives of my descendants, creating in them thoughts and ideas and desires that match Yours. Let their hearts be so full of Your living Word that when they speak from the overflow of their hearts (Luke 6:45), the words of their mouths will be the words from Your mouth (John 14:24).

24. "I will put my law in their minds and write it on their hearts. I will be their God, and they will be my people" (Jeremiah 31:33).

I pray that Your law will be encoded in the spiritual DNA of my descendants. May Your law become their instinctual and spontaneous way of living, more natural to them than unrighteousness.

25. "May your deeds be shown to your servants, your splendor to their children. May the favor of the Lord our God rest upon us; establish the work of our hands for us—yes, establish the work of our hands" (Psalm 90:16–17).

Lord, make my life Your theater—a stage upon which You perform. Through my life, may Your splendor be shown to my descendants.

26. "He revered me and stood in awe of my name. True instruction was in his mouth and nothing false was found on his lips. He walked with me in peace and uprightness, and turned many from sin" (Malachi 2:5–6).

Let these words, used to describe Levi, be true also of my descendants.

27. "You still the hunger of those you cherish; their sons have plenty, and they store up wealth for their children" (Psalm 17:14).

Lord, create in my descendants a hunger and craving for righteousness, a hunger that only You can satisfy

*(Matthew 5:6). Fill their lives so completely that they dis-
cover satisfaction only in You. Fulfill Your promise in
their lives that "I will satisfy the priests with abundance,
and my people will be filled with my bounty, declares the
LORD" (Jeremiah 31:14).*

28. "I will give you a new heart and put a new spirit
in you; I will remove from you your heart of stone
and give you a heart of flesh. And I will put my
Spirit in you and move you to follow my decrees
and be careful to keep my laws" (Ezekiel
36:26–28).

Lord, move my descendants to follow You.

29. "As the deer pants for streams of water, so my
soul pants for you, O God. My soul thirsts for God,
for the living God. When can I go and meet with
God?" (Psalm 42:1–2).

*Lord, make Yourself irresistible to my descendants,
that they will thirst for You.*

30. "'Build up, build up, prepare the road!
Remove the obstacles out of the way of my people.' For this is what the high and lofty One says—
he who lives forever, whose name is holy: 'I live in
a high and holy place, but also with him who is
contrite and lowly in spirit, to revive the spirit of

the lowly and to revive the heart of the contrite'"
(Isaiah 57:14-15).

Remove the obstacle of pride from the lives of my descendants. Create in them hearts that are meek and receptive to Your Spirit. Revive them according to Your Word.

Books by Jennifer Kennedy Dean

RICHES STORED IN SECRET PLACES:
A Devotional Guide for Those Who Hunger for the Deep Things of God

In this exciting 12-week devotional guide, Dean shows readers how to discover the layers of truth hidden in the Scriptures. Dean teaches her own methods for contemplative prayer guided by God's Word. Each week the reader will delve into a passage of Scripture and practice daily journaling/prayer/listening exercises that will start her on a lifetime journey of hearing God. Author Marilynn Carlson Webber calls this book "a modern devotional classic for today's Christian."

THE PRAYING LIFE:
Living Beyond Your Limits

With so many books about prayer, can anything new or fresh be said? Probably not, I thought, as I began to read The Praying Life. *I was happy to find this book refreshing and challenging.*
— **BOOKSTORE JOURNAL**

The consensus on this book is that it is unusually insightful, straightforward, and deep. Here Dean addresses the universal questions about prayer: If God is sovereign, why do we pray? Does prayer have an impact on the earth, or is it just a reflective activity? Is prayer more than a conversation between two parties? Dean uses imaginative and original illustrations to teach deep and biblical truths.

HEART'S CRY:
Principles of Prayer

Cynthia Heald, in her book *Becoming a Woman of Prayer* (Nav-Press), places quotes from Jennifer Kennedy Dean's book *Heart's Cry* in the company of classic thinkers and devotional writers. Each section of *Heart's Cry* deals with a scriptural principle of prayer and ends with a meditation, questions for reflection, and review questions. *Heart's Cry* is a perfect tool for personal devotionals, small-group prayer studies, and one-on-one mentoring relationships. This little book, so rich and packed with wisdom and clear biblical teaching, has already been called a classic.

New Hope
Publishers

Equipping You to Share the Hope of Christ

www.newhopepubl.com

Legacy of Prayer

Other Books by Jennifer Kennedy Dean

LIVE A PRAYING LIFE:

Open Your Life to God's Power and Provision

A comprehensive, in-depth, 13-week study. Perfect for study groups, Sunday school classes, prayer groups, and individuals. Contains interactive questions and prayer-journaling exercises.

Author Jennifer Kennedy Dean addresses the complexities of prayer with candor, intelligence, and insight. Through her own soul-quest to discover the deep truths about prayer, she has honed a message that is biblically based and theologically sound. Her skill with words combines with an imaginative and original use of illustrations to create a book that is deep, yet clear and understandable. The study is divided into four sections: The Purpose of Prayer, The Process of Prayer, The Promise of Prayer, and The Practice of Prayer.

HE RESTORES MY SOUL:

A Forty-Day Journey Toward Personal Renewal

Jennifer Kennedy Dean has discovered the secrets of the ages that transcends all religious dogma and activity—knowing and experiencing God Himself! Join her soul journey and know your Creator in a powerful and new way, and invite Him to restore your soul.

—DR. BILL BRIGHT
Founder and President, Campus Crusade for Christ International

Jennifer Dean's He Restores My Soul *offers an invaluable journey to deeper intimacy with Jesus in an insightful forty-day devotional. For those who long for renewal, spiritual refreshment, and a heart more centered on God and more receptive to His voice, I recommend this book.*

—CHERI FULLER
speaker and author of the best-selling *When Mothers Pray*,
the Gold-Medallion-winner *Extraordinary Kids*, and other books

Legacy of Prayer

HE LEADS ME BESIDE STILL WATERS:

A Forty-Day Journey Toward Rest for Your Soul

"Sabbath is not a day of the week, but a state of the soul."
This book will help you learn to live with your soul at rest.

Jennifer Kennedy Dean is a gift to the Body of Christ. I am so grateful that she has allowed God to lead her beside still waters so that she can encourage the rest of us to find our soul-rest there. Take a refreshing drink from this wonderful brook! The waters run deep!

—BETH MOORE
Speaker and author of *Breaking Free*
and *A Woman's Heart, God's Dwelling Place*

Most Christians know the soul-rest that comes from relying totally on the finished work of Christ for salvation. However, many do not know the inner rest that comes from daily relying on His strength instead of our weakness. He Leads Me Beside Still Waters *is not a book to be read, but rather a book to be experienced. For forty days, you will sit at the feet of the Master Teacher and learn the joy of inner rest.*

—GARY D. CHAPMAN, PH.D.
Counselor, marriage seminar leader, and author
of the best-selling *The Five Love Languages*

THE LIFE CHANGING POWER
IN THE BLOOD OF CHRIST

This six-week study of the blood of Christ will open your eyes to the astounding power available to every believer. Author Jennifer Kennedy Dean has an exceptional gift for seeing and explaining the depths of God's Word. If you think you've heard all there is about the blood of Christ, think again.

"Several years ago, the Spirit began to show me that there are layers of truth about the blood of Christ, and that I had only scratched the surface. I have discovered that a deeper understanding of the blood of Christ makes all the difference as we learn to walk in the power of the Spirit."

—JENNIFER KENNEDY DEAN

AWE

This enhanced CD offers both music and 30 days of interactive devotionals. These two elements lay the groundwork to create an atmosphere for the Wind of the Spirit to blow through your life in all His power.

Turn on your CD player and worship through the heart-stirring music of AWE. Now, put the CD in your computer and begin your 30-day worship experience—a journey into the deep things of God.

POWER PRAYING:
Prayer That Produces Results

Author Jennifer Kennedy Dean proves once again that the truth about prayer's power lies beyond pat slogans. While expanding our definitions of prayer and moving beyond set formulas, Dean shows that the key to consistent prayer power is in living moment-by-moment in the present-tense life of the Spirit.

CONTACT JENNIFER KENNEDY DEAN AT:
THE PRAYING LIFE FOUNDATION
P.O. Box 62
Blue Springs, MO 64013
Phone: (888) 844-6647
Fax: (816) 228-0925
jenniferkdean@prayinglife.org
www.prayinglife.org

Other Resources for Building a Legacy of Prayer

FAMILY 15

A subscription-based devotional video series that makes it easy for families to enjoy devotions with a format that engages all ages. The interactive, practical videos will get you and your family talking about the truths of the Bible through compelling 15-minute devotions. Each volume contains one 15-minute session for each week of the month. (Mention *Building a Legacy of Prayer* and receive a special discount.)

(866) 443-2614

www.family15.com

MOTHERWISE

MotherWise has become a lifeline for mothers of all ages and stages, providing the biblical instruction moms need to thrive in today's chaotic and changing society. Denise Glenn's Bible study materials take you deep into God's Word to find the answers you seek as you strive to rear godly offspring and build a solid marriage. You'll benefit from her experiences as a seasoned mother. *MotherWise* is more than study materials; it is a community of mothers networking to pray for and nourish one another in the high calling of motherhood.

1-888-272-6972 Monday–Friday,

9:30 a.m.–6:30 p.m. CST

P. O. Box 572387

Houston, TX 77257

deniseglenn@motherwise.org

www.motherwise.org

TEACHERS IN PRAYER

Teachers in Prayer for Schools (TIPS) equips teachers to make real educational reform through the use of prayer. Vicki Caruana, organizer of TIPS, encourages and inspires teachers to do what is right, teaching them to pray collectively for their students, their students' parents, and their colleagues.

www.teachersinprayer.com

FAMILIESPRAY USA

FamiliesPray USA, dedicated to encouraging the hearts of mothers, building families, and inspiring hope through the amazing power of prayer. Cheri Fuller provides articles, creative ideas and reflections in her "Mothering By Heart" series, FAQ's for MOMS (a Question & Answer format for you to ask questions about your most important or puzzling mothering issues), inspiring stories, books, and resources.

Families Pray USA/Mothering By Heart
P. O. Box 770493
Oklahoma City, OK 73177
www.cherifuller.com

MOMS IN TOUCH

Moms In Touch International is two or more moms who meet for one hour each week to pray for their children, their schools, their teachers, and administrators.

www.momsintouch.org